WHO ASKS THE CATERPILLAR

WHO ASKS THE CATERPILLAR

JEANNE ELLIN

PEEPAL TREE

First published in Great Britain in 2004
Peepal Tree Press
17 King's Avenue
Leeds LS6 1QS
England

ISBN 1 900715 96 1

Peepal Tree gratefully acknowledges Arts Council support

CONTENTS

I

KALI DANCES

A song for separation and change

Kali dances, without pity, to a rhythm that shears flesh from bone,
severing all ties. Mouth agape, she swallows touch; thirsting,
ravenous, she drains all warmth from memories, leaving
only bloodied bones as witness of loss, pain, as Kali dances,

dances, till her sinews melt. Her eyes glare red defiance of our
soft-fleshed lies. Her feet, bone-white, stamp and dance; white bone
feet dance and stamp to honour change, celebrate the truth of loss,
and please Death, who garlands her with skulls in tribute, as she

dances pain and dissolution into the world, dances her bones bare
to create again the sacred void, eternal nothing, where all might be.

ON LEAVING THE MOTHERLAND

Why is my mother here? I've become her reflection. I had, like vampires, stopped looking.
Mirrors in this country did not reflect me. Its time zone is unique. Twenty years were forever
or days. I sang some lullabies. I did not colonize, am going home to become nobody I know.
A lullaby night, singing, rocking, soothing, becoming obsolete, while five hundred years moved

crooning over my floating body, twenty thousand nights' weight ache in my girl bones – and my mother
fills my mirror. Few formalities, no half-mast flag for temporary citizens. Just surrender your passport.
No baggage allowance, no cash or credit transfer. To reduce paper work, the volunteer reorientation
programme has been cancelled. You may wish to read this helpful booklet on adjustment. You may take

only what you brought on entry. Sadly it deteriorated in storage. You will notice the change in climate.
Blood will run thin for some months. All your cold weather gear is nibbled, or gnawed but we have a
few more recent donations that are surplus. As for a nun returned to the world, girl clothes wait, mocking.
Shall I linger, clinging to an airport trolley, grating on gratuities, or leave briskly to wake to loneliness?

HOME IS A LAND

whose texture my feet have forgotten,
while my skin still holds the feel of
sweat-sliding oily pearls, when heat
baked itself into the memory of bones;

that lived only in the space between,
scribbled over with a thicker line which
grants others definition, that slowly faded
invisible unless you knew where she was;

that without births or belonging, families
slowly become the dust covering closed
registers. Unmapped her name shrivels
as exiles' tongues forget her geography.

Exhausted mother, held back from
dreamless rest by the insistent memories
of her diminishing children, she waits for
them to die into undemanding silence.

Home was

WHEN I HAVE TO ASK WHY, ASK WHY

Cell deep I am an elephant's child, why and why driven,
a mongoose running to touch rough edges, toes curling
above the abyss, needing no rationale for caring, no excuse
for passion, no permission to breathe. To know, to experience,

to go deeper is breath. But without enmeshing curiosity's
weight, a single day's slow unravelling without questions
to burr or snag, that placidity would unfold translucent
wings, that silence would prepare for a final flight.

WHEN THE BOX SHUTS ON THE SHELL

it sits like a nervous guest on a saggy sofa of cotton wool,
cleansed of its past, the last grain of sand, the daily irritation
of intimacy gone, the ozone scent of childhood bleached out,
the tactile memory of that limp, shifting moistness which

defined relationship, scuffed away. Dry. Safely dry, free of
parasites, free of tenant. Still, outside and in. Nested in white
as the lid is fitted, file number cross-indexed, case box closed.
In the cardboard-smelling dark, silence begins in the hollow

centre, spirals outwards, rinsing stroking shaping enfolding
structure. Now the shell holds only the sighing of oceans.

WHAT WE LEFT BEHIND

If someone was to pass later, sleeve the grime from the glass and peer
in, they'd see ghost rugs pale as dust, plastic chairs lapping each other
to console their rejection, a stepped-on foil dish for hedgehog's cat-food
cosied up to several urgent personal letters from Reader's Digest, and one
large shell, jetsam again, fitting the empty house like the perfect tenant.

BUT I SPEAK ENGLISH ALREADY

All my sentences finished voice up, like the questions it was rude to ask:
"Why is there no meat in this mince pie? How many times must you say thank you in a shop?
Why don't words in books mean what they say?" In the corner shop I show off my birthday presents:
new top and leggings, bright turquoise blue cotton. I ask: "Do you like my new birthday suit?"
Their laughter told me I had said something dirty.

ii: My First English Curry

Cooked by a bustling neighbour long before takeaways and late night lager-swilling
made vindaloo an English drinking ritual, cooked with good intentions – apples, raisins, bananas,

the ghosts of long-dead spices too weak to haunt my tongue with a hint of home; dressed in enough
turmeric to robe a Buddhist nun; sitting like a pool of sick on two tablespoons of claggy pudding rice –

if it's the thought that counts,
I'm glad she never tasted mine.

iii: First English School Dinner

On a thick white plate, brown-fringed lettuce, flat and wet, tomatoes leaking
jellied seeds, eggs with that boiled-too-long, shelled-too-late, olive-green tinge
to their yellow eyes, grey-faced potatoes with lumpy acned complexions,
maroon discs that I don't recognise. "Beetroot? ... And this creamy blob?

Mayonnaise?" When I discovered that beetroot bled into everything, I made
the egg and potatoes and the mayonnaise all Barbie pink. Pudding was gloppy,
white with shining blobs thunking into the bowl. "Tapocia," the dinner lady
said. "What is Tapocia?" "Toads' eggs, frogs' spawn," the boys said. I found

a silver-foil milk-bottle top in mine. Dinner lady said I'd got the lucky portion
and she gave me an extra spoon of red jam to stir in and turn it all bright pink.

WE NAKED

We who can lay no tap-rooted claim to any earth,
expect only the stranger's place at every table.
We learn confidence early, since we lack
clothes for camouflage – no family hand-me-downs.

So, naked we must be, sighing for the comfort of
conformity's small dilemmas that we cannot touch.
Our reach is greater, a family talent of those without
family, but who will teach us to play? We stay open

longer, eyes and mind. Heart is a snail's shell that
smashes stony, stubborn hope. Can smooth stone
fragments still yearn for mossy love to soften, claim
them, sheathe them into belonging earth?   Oh yes.

NEEDING INFINITY

A lifelong lover of snug spaces, yearning for a rutted path protected
by green, grown into light-sifting arches. Dreaming of shadowed
hidden places, claustrophobic with secrets. Longing for turmeric
and ochre heat to retake my bones, for sharp-edged light to make

shadows grateful, what have I to do with vast north-tinged blues,
with these hypnotic changing/unchanging movements? How has
this chill spectrum called me to unfaithfulness? I have no answer,
only that I would stand eternal,naked in this moment, my sanded

feet cold, braceleted by a blue my skin knows but my tongue can't
find a name for; I breathe infinity through thirsting eyes and skin.

MERMAID'S DAUGHTER

My mother's sisters sold their hair, bought a little knife,
oyster-sharp, pearl handle, pressed it to her palm — to cut
her free from humanity. Instead she chose "True Love",
waited for her prince, wept, kept the blade sharp. Later

cut my cord, curled my feet round its razor edge, to teach
me how to walk. Little piggies was our bedtime ritual —
but we never counted five to "catch a fish alive". She
never sang; tone or pitch might recall drowning sailors,

remind neighbours of our difference, draw cousins to slow
strangle in men's nets. Seaside holidays were vulgar,
not for a prince's child; bastards cannot risk being common.
Walking was our human heritage, dancing our ambition.

She was so proud of her feet. Salved, painted red on sole
and heel. Her ten toes, counted nightly, creamed, all ten
nails lacquered Hot Pink, Passion Pink. Dress sense was
a gauzy scarf to blur gill's shadow under chin, basque or

bustier to distract from hunt for fins. Cream, cream, cream
stubborn scales, sand-scrub them nightly. Check for fish
breath — hourly peppermint rinse. Most of all, believe; you
must believe that when you are a perfect woman dancing on

human feet, your prince will come. Step-on-step, step on
razor's edge, I learnt to dance for love, for a prince. Only
human, I stand on the pavement's edge sore footed, waiting, for
a prince. But sudden salt tang drawn in, finds me, through all

the traffic, finds me. Unused fins prickle, start erect. Gills tear
free like perineum in rapid birth. Pearl-handled knife shreds
seams. Spine flexes ghost muscles. Scales sequin edges, defeat
matt binding cream, glimmer, exuding their own unguent. Skin

melts, legs fuse in freedom. Sinewy sweep clears traffic. I breathe
a different air. In siren depths, return my aunts' small oyster knife,
still sharp, and ten painted toes.

We are the children of men and nameless siren
mothers who bequeath us sequin skin and salty
dreams. We walk among men, half-effaced, part
embraced, suspected of secreting shine and slime.

Shamemongers prick for vestigial fin or hint of
gill in crease of neck or cup of arm. We risk only
shallow breaths, half asthmatic with secrets. Fish
can never be cousin, only distanced, salt-scaled, other.

Mornings we surface, wet from tidal dreams. Spines
twitch at oddly naked base, no power-lashing tail
answers. Sealed gills ache, struggle to draw in natal
broth from this thin, early air. We leave our sheets

sequined with shed skin. Shower in dead water, churn
and spit minty rinse, to lose that briny breath. Apply
industrial deodorant guaranteed to preserve against
deep cover stress. The truth must not be sweated out.

Coal Tar anoints silver skin. Psoriasis is common,
worse under pressure. Thick soles, insoles, natural
cotton socks, make little difference, though their use
is catalogued as a sign, one of many. Detection/deception

are paired sciences. We walk on an invisible tide of
spilt ichor, solidified into the consistency of glass,
splintering at every step, piercing ball, scoring across
toes, cratering heels. We walk smiling, with that light

dancing step we learn before speech. False smile till
we say laughing, *I am child of both, a fish that speaks.*

WHO ASKS THE CATERPILLAR?

After a lifetime of voracious consuming – and I was a happy-shopper –
suddenly my appetite slackens. I no longer desire speech since I know
words that could frame this feeling would display my bewilderment,
my shame, my difference. I want privacy, silence. I curl up, wrap up

in bottomless fall – I won't call it free since this descent is fear weighted.
There are no holds for absent limbs to grasp.
Where are my arms, my legs? Mummy-wrapped into numbness,
mouth is skin sealed, eyes fogged, ears too closely swaddled to vibrate.

Every fibre unravelled, every nerve un-sleeved, I am overwhelmed
by changes, saved by mouse stillness. In this dark, bounded only by
a drumming, bone-heard rhythm, I breathe time. Time. Sensations rise
as kaleidoscope settles into an unfamiliar pattern. I don't recognise

the sensory messages or their originating codes. I am? New? Open?
Opening? Stretching? What? It quivers warming, firming in the sunshine.
No more belly crawl, no more face-down, face-filling consumption;
instead the breeze turns me into a stringless kite. I have wings but

no stomach for yesterday's food and remember an appetite I can
no longer satisfy. Scented thermals mark a flight path to a bright-petalled
port. I tongue green-gold high-octane fuel but load no cargo except
rose breath and honeysuckle exhalations. Suddenly I'm this ethereal

being, all pure pastel thoughts and flowery desires, but I'm no Buddhist,
no flower-child. I didn't sign up for this spiritual stuff. You expect me
to sacrifice my platinum card and two-hour lunches for some sticky-egged
future I will never see? One pure, blue-roofed day for my happy-munching,

money-grubbing flaming Ferrari cocktail weeks is not a fair exchange,
I know my rights as a consumer; give me back my caterpillar-minded days.

BUTTERFLY CULT

They made it sound so good, newer than Kabbalah.
Everyone is so into transformation. Avoid the fast track
to a heart attack, just sign up like that big brother celeb,
go through a sort of purification / initiation, then a world

of bright intense sensation floating free of earthbound
money-grubbing. They kept the details vague, part of
Transformation is Surrendering Control, trusting process.
I aced the cleansing fast; it was a real high and they

showered me with praise, then a small white empty
room and the silent hands wrapping and turning my
light body, wrapping scratchy thin gauze over eyes,
ears, mouth. I struggled but my hands were already tied.

In the dark, I lost time and mind. Crusted
wrappings had to be cut off. Changed. In filmy robes,
I collect offerings and mate "for the future", too refined
for pizza, chips — no stomach — but I remember having teeth.

MORNING MISSION

Enter the airlock between dream and cold
while waiting for consciousness to recycle,
test the body-suit joint by joint; extend,
contract, flex, wriggle and shrug, sinking

deeper with each breath; call the nerve
connections, scroll up recorded reflexes,
flush out stale residues of night briefing,
shred scraps of symbols that might compromise.

You can hope to return to what is just behind,
barely out of grasp. But seal your mind now,
there must be no seepage; that mix is too rich
for skin-suited consumption. Checks complete.

On the count of three move out into daily space,
sealed into body-suit, umbilical still trailing.

NAME THIS CHILD

This colourless midnight light fulfils empty promises to the vacant letter of an absent dictionary.
It holds the form of trees captive without feeling for their hungers, denying their need to rootle
deep in decent dark-fed dreams, glassing their life in light-stasis until the hot truth rises banishing
the photocopy. Some of us follow this cold, moon-diminishing light, preferring its predictable frame,

observing life as neighbours from within another culture. Some endow this Highland summer night
with sinister tones, weight it with childish dreams of otherness back-lit by hermaphrodiac twilight,
use its cool pallid surface to paint our own fears or embrace its not quite darkness as manageable risk.
But there is another view of this strange child disowned by parent day, estranged daughter of dark. Judged

by either standard she is neither, and can never satisfy until we change the chromatic scale to make
between another colour, name this shade without defining reference, except to its own intrinsic quality.

THE GUILTY PART

I thought it was a sort of gland everyone was born with, like original sin,
somehow necessary for health but very prone to overflow. The way to control
its secretions was self-doubt, applied twice daily, toothpaste with a limited
choice of flavours — abrasive abject, or corrosive hyper (relaxed only worked

before teeth emerged and began to encounter complex solid foods). Regular
weekly confession provided scale and polish, with drilling questions to flush
our gritty details of decay. Exactly which impure thoughts? How often did you
invite, entertain or detain them? Have you avoided the occasions of sin?

How do you plan to do so in the future? Do you have a firm purpose of amendment?
I had wonderfully firm purposes at seven. The departure of the tooth fairy started
the rot. Puberty affects the guilt-gums, changes the quality and flow of saliva too —
taste buds rampant, running riot, diluting, masking guilt's acidic secretions.

When it was time for root canal work I abandoned dental hygiene, but not sweets,
harboured a faint regret for the mildly antiseptic ritual mouth-wash and peppermint
feeling on my tongue, adding fresh appreciation to new tastes, but learnt that salt and
soot make a substitute for tooth powder. I bought my own angled mirror and found that

hard sinewy meats provide a full-floss dental plan. Took an x-ray of the guilty
gland and read its original bar code. Implant removed, but sometimes I feel it twitch.

AS A PRECAUTION I NEVER WALK BAREFOOT IN CHURCH

Guilt is easily communicated through bare feet padding innocent across religious mosaics.
Tender soles are most vulnerable. Early infection is tenacious. Conventional treatment doesn't
seek to eradicate, only accommodate the thickening hyper-sensitized tissue in goody two shoes
with bars, buckles and laces, moulding feet into reliance on shoe-fitters, podiatry and chiropody.

Large, bare, thick-skinned soles spread in freedom are derided as original sin waiting to be
properly shod into respectable numbness. My freed feet have spread, widened their horizons,
relish variety of textures – grass, pebbles, sand, gravel, carpet, toweling, cork, marble – even shoe
leather – without toes curling like scolded children, but as a precaution I don't walk barefoot in churches.

ANOTHER STAR

I looked every night, trying to know that he was up there,
seeing me, still daddy. Other days I searched for him in
every strange man's face; perhaps he'd sent a message.
I knew where he was buried, but we'd moved so far,

how could he find us when he stopped being dead?

NASTURTIUM

Truant from garden's easy neglect, freedom and random growth
have given it an exotic air. Un-cosseted it clings to erosion-poor,
shifting soil. Celebrates struggle by lifting bright faces to stinging
salt winds, flourishing in newly conquered habitat. What, I wonder,

do cliff-dwelling insects make of this new food? Or have garden
colonies faithfully followed, to make a tamed verge, a little suburb,
rather than a dangerous edge, where the familiar transforms and life
must earn space, without sponsorship, without utility or harvest.

II

TIME'S PASSENGER

This courtship has lacked gifts, at least on your part.
I have given and you call your taking repossession,
accuse me of carelessness with what was only lent.
My shoulders stiffen, reluctant, beneath your hands.

You murmur that I was always meant to be yours,
born to lie breathless in your arms, one with you,
completely. Your unwelcome whispers diminish all
other voices. I can't ignore your soft insidious breath

moving the hairs on my neck; your touch melts my
flesh and shrivels my skin. My secrets are old news
to you, informing your caresses, meeting your desires
as they mute mine. Marks of your passion are boldly visible:

brown brands that stand proxy for the erotic purple of
earlier kisses. My pulses slow, the rhythm of my heart
moves and changes, adapting to your proximity. My hair
bleeds colour under your fingertips, a long seduction

that can only end with my consent. So much foreplay
and still I am not ready. Not ready to join the endless
list of your lovers, sated and discarded in a heartbeat.
But I know we will have our breathless moment.

ALMOST A LOVE POEM FROM AN OYSTER

Your love is like
a picnic – wicker basket china plates – but
all the food is painted papier-mache and
tastes only of old bones and bad air.

Your love is like
a gas fire – wood veneer coal effect – but
that little red bulb has finally blown and
I've no more coins to fill your meter.

Your love is like
a show house of secret Barbie dreams but
too many others have tramped through and
tomorrow will bring me repossession

Your love has been
a handful of grit rubbed in my eyes but
my pearls are all real and so I can thank you.

YOURS FOR MINE

I return yours, gift-wrapped still; there never were any batteries supplied.
That is all, we are done and neither of us mentions the fragments lying
between us. Mine, but only a shell was shattered. Some seeds need more
than rain, an almost killer frost, passage through another's life. Rarer still

are those roused only by flame, life that must begin in ashes. Your gift
to me the knowledge that I belong to a fire-start species. Knowledge is
power; I gave mine away. Now I sift a phoenix egg from the ashes.
It glows, lambent. My breath expels to cool the weight in my hands.

DUTY KEEPS AN OPEN PRISON

Parole a daily option with hourly struggle refused.
Prisoner-jailer the keys' weight distorts my stance.
Doors close solidly on options as slow days pile up
featureless as dust, cinching chest, clogging airways.

Hope without a visiting order has found another fool.
Love or something that wears its logo'd overalls is here.
Love changes nothing, moves and is moved by nothing.
Love feels the cold. Love is? Slopping out.

LOVE CAN BE PAPER-THIN.

After so much turmoil I dare not build in brick — labour and capital exhausted by our grinding on each other. Every day I make a new home with paper walls. Hope makes a thin and short-lived glue, while torn paper recycles nicely. Sunny days, I draw some comfort on the walls, trace patterns for carpet and curtains.

The house might stand, slightly crumpled, for two days or three, then it's shaken by hailstone words or dissolved in the salt scattered to give safe footing across the frozen silences. Thaws bring other risks. If we move towards each other over these foundationless floors, we could fall fathoms and not be thrown a line.

AND IF MY LOVER WERE THE SEA

Reduced to domestic scale he'd be a pail of stale salt water, slowly
degrading. Immersed totally in him, I'd be a sack of saggy, sodden flesh.
So I'll visit as *I* choose, risk flood or absence, content if our time and tides
combine. Then enjoy, wade, drift wide, wonder, float and leave him.

Leave lightly, skin sliding a slow goodbye. Leave his bed slowly, pleasure
weighted, the wind shivering along my salted flesh, hair passion-clotted,
dripping in seaweed hanks between my shameless shoulders. Leave him to
pragmatic gulls and anoracked treasure-seekers bonded blindly to their wands.

Leave him and ask no questions of those other shores he moves towards
as I dream smiling in a deep duvet'd bed, of my other tempered seas.

NOT LOSING BUT LETTING GO

Abandoning all that, I open my veined hand,
allowing the clutched and crumpled to unfold
and find its own gravity. Since I no longer
assign weight to daily detail, history fades

without recall, fabric frayed beyond regret. I
widow memory and do not mourn. Light and
winnowed of sadness, I float as a dust mote, drift
whimsical on instant eddies, tides without moon.

Anchor is shifting on rusty chains; hear grinding
arthritic movement as it prepares for flight.
Air my new medium, I must shed weight,
abjure love that strains against lifting wind.

You stand aching, bewildered, but not unloved,
yearning for my past when love spoke. Now
you must watch me cast off, without cargo.
Yes, I am ready for flight; featherweight flies.

ARCHITECT

Wearing my skin-walled room, trying to shrink deeper inside, shutting the windows on touch, slamming the door that lets words through is not enough. He still intrudes. Make the walls secure, watch what comes in, control it, weigh it; this floor won't support another mouthful. Traitor urges rumble, *We have to compromise*. Food can be fooled into lending flavour without

furnishing calories. Call security, throw up, clean up. Keep the room neat, unfussy, safe again. Skin walls let in draught. Layer embossed papers to protect against draughty eyes and words. Paint protects against finger smears. Inch the door open, risk corridor, retreat, return slowly. Extend into a terraced house of dusty Lego bricks; strip walls, sand floor and fit patio doors.

EDGES

Where the familiar transforms, possibilities shift without promises, without lies.
Uneasy spaces between carriages, my favourite place to travel. Spread feet, body
free to move, balance constantly changing. Really feeling the ride, and always
the chance that things will shift from safe commuter trance, into unchoreographed life.

I like edges, perhaps because they are outside the rules. A train that does not always
take you home. No signposts, no one to ask. No right to know here. My life is edges.
I've lost my guarantee. No safety. No itinerary. No seat on this journey. An empty
refreshment trolley barges and bangs as it struggles past, jarring me out of a hopeful dream

to notice wooden fence posts silvered with neglect, bent into sketches of their purpose.
All I have is the view, the sensational ride, and the anticipation of a surprise ending.

SOLITUDE

Solitude slides cool about my flanks, not parting
but merging, grain and nap smoothed into their
nature and mine. House beats in small sounds
slowing my heart into syncronicity. We become

time's measure. Light moves, greeting windows,
walls, me. Silhouetted wind shivers, learns from
shadows, hears everything without words that I
forget to shape. Careful shepherd night folds

me safely. Darkness strokes me. I stretch, purr,
breathe through skin, anticipating stars' touch.

EX SINGLE PARENT BUILDS AN ARK

Silence rattles my empty ears as they depart,
thought dissolves into primal salt water. Since
this is not the Nile's fertilizing deluge, I must
become an Ark builder. Single parents learn

to handle anything, mangled cat prey or falling
ceilings, bath-obsessed spiders or midnight drunks
booting our front door. I don't have time for
seasoning timber so I build a canoe with remnants

of several half-finished model kits and parcel tape.
Have the waters receded? I know the protocol. I
did have a pair of street-grimed pigeon passengers,
also two cats, but forgot a tin opener so must pioneer.

Decay steams in the sun. I hope the worms and
dung beetles, such undemanding passengers, won't
feel overfaced, cast as Adams and Eves in a damp
paradise under reconstruction. Release two, no

fourteen rabbits, broody hens with polyglot clutches,
ducks, chicks, geese, pregnant pot-bellied pig, plus
uninvited guests — mice, fleas, woodlice. No rainbow
promises, but I find enough fragments to make peace.

MY NAME IS JEANNE, AM I STILL A POET?

Our last, carefully polished, baby has backpacked off. And
nothing. Not a word from you. Was last time the last time?
I haunt surgeries and clinics with the other barren, bereft and
infertile, all of us hunting your features in each baby. Talking

D.N.A. and blood tests. Willing to crudely dissect and flay to
prove the other's poem a bastard. Am I still a poet? Should I
stop *Poetry Review*? Resign from the group? Miss workshops,
avoid that proud new poet you've impregnated, or set the Critic

Support Agency on their tail? I don't expect fidelity, make
half apologies for blind encounters with look-alikes in your
absence. You are prolific but they can't all be your lovers. An
equal opportunities seducer; is it just willingness you want?

Then why I am still waiting? Or can I hope that you have
discrimination, value commitment... Then on a bus, or waking
puffy-eyed, words shape round gritty flecks: mica or gold?
Now it's over, without promises, when will I have your number?

Silence, dry silence. My name is Jeanne, I haven't written a
word for six weeks. I am poet. I hope I'm not in recovery.

FINITY'S DANCE

I've entered finity dressed in brightness, accepted freedom.
Green, I'd never have dared the wind, danced with this abandon.
Finity gives meaning. Earth calls time, whispers, "Choose: dance
or shrivel. Choose your death." I embrace a cold seductive force

that cries "Let go! Can't you feel that your brittle veins are ready
for one last vital surge?" I loosen my grip, seeking nothing beyond
this season. I leap into sinewy air, a bruising, vital partner. Finally
finding courage, only now living, dance till music sighs to silence.

NAME POEMS

i: After the Divorce I Dreamt Your Name Was Grain

Corn-man came wearing green, his eyes
a feral gold with cat pupils.
He demanded single combat.
We struggled, he died. I buried
him without marker. His children
sprint towards the sun, becoming mine
filling my freezer with gold eyes
linking every mouthful to him.

ii: My Real Name Is Chop

I thought my name was lost,
I had been called beloved,
I dreamed of being found.
Being searched for I felt valued
above those who had never strayed.
Beloved again I frisked in his pastures.
Tomorrow the harvest is gathered.
The promise will be redeemed
I will be one with the beloved.
My real name is Chop.

iii: Yesterday My Name Was Brave

I was strong and knew the answers. I imagined the reasons.
There were rules I kept and did and waited. In the silence
that came after I thought of what was never said. Formed
questions there was no one to answer. Good questions

and I can never know their answers. Today my name is
Has Survived. Tomorrow my name will be Open To Question.

iv: Today My Name Is Athletic

At first I thought it was a cosmic, caustic comment,
then I realised that not all muscles are blood fed.
All that owning and shouldering, all that choosing
and bench-pressing consequences have built mass.

Early gymnastics with conscience and confession
developed flexibility. Single parenting, self-employment
are excellent for cardio-vascular work and stamina.
I have run moral marathons and ethical cross-countries.

Smiling and surprised I see an athlete in my mirror. These
Olympics will never be televised but I've won my golds.

WICK MONUMENT

She stands, half blind to the sea's seven blues, as stones fade indigo waves.
Light spangles over lead and ochre cliffs, flows round offcuts of land still
ragged with lichens. Occasional white surge moves underlying flocculant
green in and out of focus, like ghost grass, while rubbing foam half reveals

an echo beneath brightest blue of patient flesh she shares with cliffs. At her
rooted feet, grasses — seedful, glossy — toss their manes, while she — dumpy,
obstinate, hopeless, memorial — stands through bone-pale nights and day-
long dusks, waits. Wants what they say she can never have, touch of her sons.

So she stands, last post, as sea and sky mark time. Waves turn to splinters of
glass, deadly glitter, steel under gunship clouds. "Too many to name," they
say. But she remembers bone of her stone. They have simply named dying
places, a litany with its own muffled drum: Corunna, Gabon. Kagdagar,

Chitrai, Alma, the Nile, South Africa, Lucknow, Zululand, Campertown,
Afghanistan, Trafalgar, the Baltic, the Noir, Toulouse, Waterloo,
Salamanca, Inkerman, Balaclava, Sebastopol. They built the widow's walk
with no access, windows as indentations. "Since," they said, "there will be

nothing to see." Snow curdles on waves' sluggish dishwater; horizon with
strong silver break; below condolence-letter grey. Time grinds small, smaller.
Rivers run, as they must. Green surprises cliffs. Sky, still cloud-wrapped against
spring chill, gentles remembering waves, as sea brings their dust to her feet.

III

MOTHER VERB AND NOUN

First:
I could have led a parade proud-belly-naked as goddess incarnate, accepting rose-petal applause.
Hubris.
Then the tide left silver drag-lines on my shriveled beach belly. With wet breasts, dry eyes, I became
ghost behind glass.

Second:
I couldn't breathe, till her first exhalation. She was a gift I could not claim, lacking grace, only serve.
I became a female thing, birth savage, ready to tongue clean, sated on her sleeping-milk smell.

Third:
She was wrenched into life, so nearly not. All night I held her one-armed, singing half-known hymns of utter
thanks for her compressed blue face, eyes full of calm curiosity. Alive.

Grief was a conduit for love, a measure against which everything else was relative.

LOST LETTER

Paper-grey sea closely written with lines of regret in a language
I cannot sound. Sheet after sheet rolls out blurred with constant
folding and unfolding of the tide. As they come closer I squint
and strain to focus. I must be able to read it. I've filled so many

notebooks with it in my dreams, but without a bilingual dictionary...
.... the light is shifting, paper rolling out in waves faster
than my lame attempts to read, to snatch a fragment of meaning
from the script before the tide blots all sense against the rocks.

EVERY DAY A TONGUE DIES

Sounds lie balanced on the breath of their last born
speaker, neglected gristle between loosening teeth,
sibilants shrinking against receding gums, glottal
stops curled defensive under tongues taught to be global.

Jobs and clean shirts, internet access, shoes found in
world village, priced in lingua franca. Walk a mile in
my branded trainers, become a citizen of the world, second class.
Forget those feelings your grandmother had a word for.

View Disney sunsets, in an American accent, and fail
the mystery of pearl-bronze mist veiling private dawns.
Beijing to Boston, universal burger is reliable brand,
spices preselected, unmoved by local winds demanding

subtle sharpness or sinuses aching for fierce heat. I can
reinvent cooking, grind massala mix, trust nose and tongue,
but how do I make the desiccated, pinned butterfly of oral tapes
plump to living gloss and waft a shimmer of multiple meanings?

MOON VIEWING

Moon presses her haloed face against a clouded window
gazes into our bottomless eyes. Wonders at the iridescent
thoughts flickering. Flying-fish thoughts skimming, leaping, diving
before our brain's coarse mesh can net them with words.

Our mystery holds her spellbound. Patient as an angler on
a river bank. She watches. Waiting for a finer woven net.

ADOPTED TONGUE

What would my mind have been with another tongue to father
my thoughts? But, posthumously born, I can only shape adopted words
heavy with unformulated longing for that other speech unsounded,
yearn for the lost words to a song that can never be written.

In my lifetime two old Chinese women destroyed the last written
pages in an ancient women's language, determined that those words
would die between their locked jaws. What poems, jokes and stories
have we lost? Worse, what words to shape a female experience – like

the rich snow vocabulary of the Inuit – are beyond echo-reach,
ashes of that fire haunting us like children never conceieved.

INFECTIOUS

I am coming down with an attack; I can feel it itching.
Only words can soothe that ragged edge of a question,
a shard whose colour I can feel under my tongue.
It hovers, getting heavier in my bones like flu.

No cure except lobotomy, so I've learnt to "manage
my symptoms". Don't try to scratch it out raw and
bleeding. Leave it. Cover the itch with the calamine
of washing and shopping, turn my compost heap,

feed my worms, snug in their tower. Then, contrary,
like a broody hen who has laid outside the coop,
a line of words emerges, still fuzzy-edged, all present
but in random, broken order, to be gently chivvied,

dried and smoothed into their right shapes by hands
blindly feeling patterns before my mind can see.

NIGHT WITHOUT SONG

Under the bed, my aspirational guitar sleeps coffined in plastic; handfuls of dust hold it in stasis.
Four a.m. visits me again; as a good host I offer world service music and coffee, since this guest will
stay until threatened by the breakfast stampede — no trace when the lunch box clamours, the sports kit,
sullen with muddy defeats clogging its seams and pores, sulks behind the utility room door,

the table dance of toast and cereal jerks to its unsatisfying climax. To work, suited and heeled, as if
I'd never had that secret assignation. Suit fronts meetings, mediates, investigates; heels attempt to
elicit hope in interviews, star in an old pre-talkie movie, waiting for guitar music to be laid down
as a sound track. Cocoon home wrapped in radio plays, seat-belt released by final credits.

Briefcase and pager stay booted. Empty pockets of day's small changes; eat soap-wrapped meal;
conduct homework audit; chase up bedtime deadlines; watch news; brush teeth; weigh down mattress;
resign from day. Lie, turn turning, and watch seconds changing, miss some hours without realising.
Thinned duvet-sleep barely covers wash-bleached dreams as uneasy head wrinkles, flattens pillows,

awaiting four am, while drug-free guitar sleeps like dead wood in soundproofing dust. Does it still
dream in Technicolor, or remember cradling arms, head bent, intimate, intent hands reaching for music?

WHEN SHE WAS FINALLY GIVEN WORDS AND LIGHT

(Channel 4 'Wild Child' Monday 15 /12/03)

The family shell was cracked. She was lifted from a world of blinkered light,
birthed into rooms with horizons and noisy windows the sun could scream
through, to live in spaces she could almost fill. They peeled the silence from
her skin like plaster, in one bright sound that widened eyes and let her bones

breath sun and space, giving a birthday thirteen years late for candle wishes.
She was brooded by linguists, egg-bound with theories to hatch, filling her
cupped palms with the bright bubbles they mouthed, words that she tongued
till they burst empty in her mouth. They found no frost-ripened potential from her
winter days, no resilient seeds of fire-start speech, only a fossil of her future loss.

Somewhere in thirteen years of wombless waiting, a soundless moment froze,
leaving language as part-blind noises, echoes of that first silence cracked too late.

CHIMPANZEE'S SONG

(In response to a television programme about the rehabilitation of a chimpanzee raised solely by humans, and her introduction to a baby chimpanzee, the first she had even seen.)

I am?

A gently caged freak with hair-covered skin and teeth too large to smile discreetly,
nervously monitoring a super-strength grip, unable to speak the only language
I can remember hearing. They are my troop, my family and I'm their grateful,
speechless fosterling. I have stopped growing, but I still watch the grownups.

One morning will I wake belonging?

Then the bold baby, demanding to be held, smelt, touched without hesitation.
I'd learnt touching on their fragile frames, a clumsy, guilt-hinged intimacy
returned in flat tones and polyester textures that made me wrong until
that small hairy hand showed me they'd always spoken prose to a poet.

How naked they are.

Those thin stiff lips that I coveted, with their narrow hedge of flabby
teeth too weak to threaten us, I could smile now to think of wanting that.
His teeth belong in that ape-strong jaw and so do mine. I make sounds
like his and we are -- smelling, touching -- meanings they are excluded from.

His rightness consecrates my own

SHOULD WE WAKE THIS STONE-WRAPPED SLEEPER?
(For the Sleeping Lady of Malta)

How generous to lie entombed, drawing silence like bedclothes round her.
What sound less powerful than that first creative word would have the weight
to break her dream, release her from millennial night to our diminished day?
And when that sound was shaped, risking a new creation,
what muscular dawn would dare to fanfare morning to her opening face?

And will she wake to complete a project planned before the sun
first heated Egypt's pride or Celtic stones stood to mark the years?
Did she lie too long? Are those who waited for her only patient dust?
Or did she dream of carrying her riddle to a strange day
peopled with motherless souls, hungry for a sacred mystery,
journeying in blind trust that, lacking a common tongue or even light of mind,
one distant morning, with her tongue bound, hemmed by the closed ears of those
with no memory of her speech, her silent stone would speak to our bones?

MENDI NIGHTS

Clustering sisters, cousins, friends wondering who'll be next, cherishing,
chattering aunts, fluttering fussing; I'm the flower to their bee-dance.
My mother's smile wavering proud, her eyes' fading suns shining on me;
I am beautiful in their smiles, polished by their tenderness.

I am precious, wrapped in their giggles and whispers, the still centre
of all this. I am painted and patterned with promises. Flowers stroked petal
by petal into garlands – they will fade these bridal flowers, but so gently it'll
be impossible to name the day their final shadow leaves my skin.

Girl secrets are tickling my ears; my friends and cousins whisper into
the shells drawn on my hands, their words spiralling into the curves of
colour while the aunties' blushing advice curves like vines up my arms,
leaves half-unfurled, half-murmured, teasing, waiting for my cheeks to flush.

Lattices snaking up from my feet – the frames of windows I've yet to look
through – promise another landscape, different weather under another
roof. The henna cone swirls a giant Persian raindrop and fills it with delicate
forms curled like sleeping children. Dreams raised in darkest green.

Hopes set under the stiffening surface. I hold myself still to take them crisp-
edged into my marriage, where they will sink beneath my skin and wait.

II

A secret ochre sea sweeps through dreams and memories.
See its drag-lines through time and geography; it rose to
mark its first level in the caves of Ajanta. Look where it
dashed against the rosy breasts of Knossos. See the warrior

beards of Afghanistan acknowledge its power. The Pharaoh's
pampered women floated their hair in its waters and spread
their bright waves to dry in the sun while the Pharaoh's toes
and fingers were hennaed, dipped to prepare for a rosy afterlife.

Restless as any azure ocean this ochre wave runs outlining
continents, defining borders, carrying for a century or ten
some brief symbol we call traditional before letting it sift
softly from memory, carrying with equal ease fresh shapes

and today's dreams till they become tomorrow's erased lines
or the cherished fragments of a fractured past.

III

Its true canvases are the shifting sands of skin, holding for a moment a pattern to be enjoyed
like the graceful turn of a dancer's head or a breathless leap from a trapeze, the spontaneous
gasp of delight made by an enthralled audience, the moment of shared silence in a darkened theatre:
moments that ebb below our surfaces, returning to their secret source, leaving the tracery of river deltas
haunting our skins' brief memory. This moment won't return, but perhaps another will draw a fresh device.

V

Not since my mother towelled my hair dry have I felt that gentle intimacy of task and trust.
History fills my palm; these lamps in their boat-like simplicity have lit homes for millennia –
Inuit, Roman, Eustruscan, Hindu – and this five-petalled daisy filling each finger tip is universal
flower as the rayed circle is sun – a language written in skin in celebration and in reminder of

what we share: the briefness of breath, the turning from tears to laughter, from promise to hope.
There is no living skin on whose surface *that* could not be written truthfully, to net us all
in one web, the shapes black and raised like the track of puffer pens. The ripening itch beneath must
be resisted, that childhood urge to pick a scabby knee revisited. I resist and keep my hand

unsoaked or soaped and it reveals itself dark ochre, filling my palm, turning my skin into
an embroidered fabric. I cup and crease my palm to see the pattern change but it is my hand
that is new. I am an embroidered woman, cousin to Maori and those who wear needle pictures
on back or belly. I have a visitors visa to the country of the decorated people; I am gazed at too.

I AM UNDER THE WATER

Your pebble words fall
        towards me,
               through brown and grey,
                rinsed of meaning
                    before they touch my liquid ears
with broken, half-familiar rhythms
              that tease fading senses
                  into response.
                        Fish mouth purses air
                that rises towards you,
                    fragile, beautiful.
                              It surfaces, releasing emptiness.

                              I am rippling
           in the wash of your movements.
                        I make none.
        Letting the water speak.

IV

BLAME SPRING FLOWERS

I know I shouldn't have — worn last year's sun dress, gone out without my training bra,
forgotten my sports kit, dawdled through the park on the way to school, run
shoeless across the grass to pick the flowers. That's why He came sudden and scary,
the bogey man we thought lived in the dark under the stairs. But I wasn't pretending.

I screamed. My friends ran as he pulled me into the molasses darkness, grave dark,
to force ripeness like Christmas bulbs stored under the stairs. No one moved to help me. His
eyes were hot, his tongue too big for my mouth. He didn't speak, just grabbed with hard
hands. In the dark no one saved me. I was buried in secrets. My mouth too dry to tell,

jaw clamped too tight to swallow. Anyway, hell is too full of lies to eat. I should have
kicked and bitten, called louder, hoped longer, but He said no one would come. He said
I was his little queen, his baby-wife. I said: "I want my mother!" When they came
to take me home he seemed sad, asked me to please eat something before I left. I took a

bite of shrivelled fruit to be polite. The judge said that meant something. Like my
too small sundress and trespassing barefoot on the grass, picking flowers, dawdling to
school. They didn't say anything about forgetting my sports kit. Since it was partly
my fault I have to spend time sharing his sentence. I suppose that's fair. I am fine

in spring and summer; I dance barefoot in floaty, flirty skirts. Autumn starts a different
cycle. Don't mention Him. It is Seasonal Affective Disorder. Or you can just say sad.

MOTHER WILL

I couldn't believe she'd gone, vanished as if the ground had opened and swallowed her.
I searched, my eyes blank, called till voice was a bloody stub. Gave pathetic interviews.
Sleepless, sodden, gummy-eyed. "Just bring her back, please." What else could I say?
But there was no help. Politics and jurisdictions. They said I didn't grasp the nuances.

Right, I was slow. Power is a simple exchange of threats, favours. Slow, but I grasped it
in the end. His power held the balance, so he reframed rape: *diplomatic discretion, oiling
commerce, too complex to explain, security*. I should get on with my life, go back to work,
be productive, not hysterical. They offered, but I shut my ears to counselling. I won't adjust.

I need power, not adjusting. What is power? I had none. Soft handed. Soft, empty hands.
Crops failed. Cattle starved, fruit fell rotten, vegetables curled brown, dried while I wept.
Did nothing. Their polls bottomed. Governments fell. Suddenly, rank by rank, ascending
smooth-voiced suits came, with threats first, then well-packaged guilt, chocolate-coated

to appeal to girly taste. No appetite; not tempted. Stone steady. Only one demand: my girl.
Give me back my daughter. Bigger, better offers, sweeter words, then chocolate off the guilt.
I did not bite. Cars, white goods, villa holidays, jewellry, game show prizes. No negotiation
skills. I just sit, granite mother waiting for her daughter. Finally they agree. She is free.

Even then they cheat, insert last minute small print. Six seeds, a sentence and her coronation.
Queen of hell half of every year. In exchange I give them the cold fruitlessness of winter.

It is all about that quiver. That tightening, loosening flow
of excitement and a man who is just contained danger.
It never lasts, of course. But always another, generating
that quiver, the satisfaction of containing, controlling violence,

rendering it flaccid. Playing whore, or princess, whispering,
laughing in moist darkness at jokes and wit short-lived as
passion. Of course I'm familiar. You know me. I'm the teenage
girl who thinks with her nerve endings, riding hormonal surf

on a fragile board. I'm the woman always looking for love over
the shoulder of the man she's with. Excitement and danger
don't pay bills. But somehow they get paid. Always someone
with an eye for petty detail. Does respect and efficiency heat

your blood? No? Nor mine. I need new desire heated to scalding
in stranger's eyes. When I'm old would be time enough for
friendship with a man. But I'm immortal. Men are my mirror,
faces blind-burnished with lust showing me that I am beautiful.

Settle down? Not while there is a man left unsampled. Trophy wife,
my votary, may briefly mirror me, borrow for an hour my garment
of rosy flesh, always poised at ripe. I have nothing to say to placid
domesticity, till a house raises blind, mindless desire. Husbands

I've had. One was mine. Kind, yes; tried to keep me with hard
work and gifts. Burned, smouldered with jealousy. What did he
expect? Netted me with my lover, my war-machine, hot, bloody,
who becomes a sleeping boy in my arms. Oh that marine buzz-cut,

stimulating and tender to touch, vulnerable nape exposed. Throat
hoarse with battle yells, made to groan in surrender. Tangy, fresh
flowing sweat, oiling over skin sun-reddened, but still tender pale
in secret places opened to me. Time not lost in the blind dazzle

of desire is lost time. My beauty, constantly renewed in wide-eyed
heat, armours against the glacier flow of a fathomless fear.

THE FIRST MISUNDERSTOOD HUSBAND/ABUSED WIFE?

"This week's show: *Jealous wives — harridans or heroines?*"

"Our first guest suffers from pathological jealousy. She's hired detectives,
set dogs to follow her husband, prevented one of her rivals from receiving
medical attention, hounded her from place to place while she was pregnant
with twins — leading to her giving birth alone after a difficult labour.
But she says she's the victim to be pitied. Let's meet her. Come in, Hera." (Boo Hiss)

"Oh I know what you think: sad possessive stalker. Easy to mock an
ageing, jealous wife, know me only for that shameful, misdirected rage.
His nymphs, dryads, semi-demi-goddesses, sisters, nieces, cousins, all
immortals with eternity to smirk at me over their ambrosia, his pretty boy

pouring our wine and smiling sweetly: these I bear. If I began to complain
in our family, who knows what could unravel. We can use endless time to
offend and forgive. Respect? Now there's a pitfall, cite that to a parricide
who mated his sister by force. So I smile and preside, Queen of Heaven,

mother of gods, wife to the father of all. But I will not accept this ceaseless
procession of mortal minxes, each preening herself on seducing a god.
Do they think he will treat a passing itch with more tenderness than the
Queen of Heaven? Can they really believe promises broken before the breath

that carries them is dispersed? How little it takes to engage him. A few ounces
of rosy flesh, bouncing. Thick tangles wantoning over sulky shoulders. They
claim rape, compulsion; then why do they ask favours, showers of gold, beg
for god-children, demand to be hidden from me?"

"Why have you put up with it? Haven't you told him what you think of his behaviour?"

"I have raised voice and hand against him. Yes, and carried the bruises of his reply
on my white arms, my woman's body. A goddess can bleed. Still I complained,
cried aloud my rage and pain. Reproached him. In reply he manacled wrists
and ankles, dangled me in the void between earth and heaven. Now I am silent.

His threats speak unbroken promises. His blows echo in my bones like words.
'Let no god or goddess attempt to curb my will or…' No one doubts his power.
So I live with the presence of his preferred second wife, whose opinion he seeks
before mine. Know about his other children, his seduction/ rape of my sister Demeter.

A thin line with him; say yes or no, he'll have what he desires. Ask Aegina, Alcemne, Callista, Danae, Europa. And wives? Ask Metis, swallowed alive, her daughter unborn. Even her motherhood denied as he gave birth to daddy's girl, Athena.

"Wow. You seem like a real messed up bunch."

"A dysfunctional family? Yes. Patricide, infanticide, incest, rape, kidnap, assault, adultery, domestic violence, theft, deception: you can apply labels to our actions, but beware, if you no longer worship: do not presume to judge."

"How does it feel to have your wine poured by your husband's boy-lover?"

"Bitter."

"Why did you marry him?"

"Do they teach you nothing now? He came powerful, golden, demanding and I refused – refused my brother fresh from killing our father. He transformed into a shivering bird seeking my body warmth for very life. Compassion opened my arms and he took his true form. I resisted, bargained. A wife must have more status than a rape victim, I thought."

"We should give Zeus his say, after all we've only heard one side of the story. I believe we have him on the phone…"

"Hera is my wife. I've given her that status, and respect – jewels, credit cards: she has everything any reasonable woman could want. She is a perfect hostess and queen except for hysterical overreaction. I am a very human god, I have my little flaws. A pout or two, a thrown cup – tempests that could be mended with promises and presents – I wouldn't

grudge her that much satisfaction, but she goes too far. Bloodhounds and spies, public rants; it feeds the tabloid piranhas, detracts from the important achievements of my administration. It sets such poor example for mortals. They need to see dignity and restraint in the public manners of their gods. I work hard; I need domestic harmony.

Which of you miserable mortal men would live patiently under jealous scrutiny? Who could expect that of me? I am more god than any god, with all the attributes of a man. Any man will, if he is honest, tell you that fidelity is overrated by women, by goddesses, too, for that matter. These little detours mean nothing. A sneeze that they magnify into

marital pneumonia. Surely it is the long view women should take. They have so much more to lose. But if you insist on counting fidelity, I have been more faithful than any man.

All three hundred years of our honeymoon, I was faithful. Three hundred years and then a few little incidents — that would have been nothing if she'd made nothing of them.

Yes I lost my patience, raised my voice to drown her screeching. Tried to tease her out of her overreactions. Perhaps setting up a mock bridal procession was a little unkind, but it worked. She attacked the mock bride and came back home. Threats? Only to get her to behave reasonably. I do regret the slap; I should have been patient, treated her hysteria

more conservatively. Silence about these domestic details would have been more dignified for her, but she does have this dramatic tendency. Bruises? That fine white skin she's so proud of marks with a breath, a calming grip, a shake. Like her it exaggerates. If I'd abandoned my children, that would be something to nag about. I acknowledge all mine —

whoever their mothers happen to be, I take care of them — but even that virtue she holds against me. There's no satisfying her. Still, eternity would be bland without her. Our little disagreements add spice. She knows I always come back to her. She's a worn in pair of slippers, a good wife — or she would be if she'd just ease up on the jealous act…"

"Thank you Zeus, now the woman in the red tee shirt ?"

"Why not leave the bastard? Go to a refuge or something?"

"I have run and been tricked, trapped or enticed back. Nowhere to run, I return. Where could I hide from all-seeing Zeus? He has the powers of monsters on call. I have no domain, no rule, and no powers outside his reach. I am Hera, wife of Zeus. That is all I am, wife. Betrayed wife, jealous, ageing wife, fading, helpless wife,

ranting , spying, prying wife. Even my pets mirror my obsession. My many-eyed dog, Argus, lives to watch him. My multi-pupilled peacock fan hardly cools my rage. He no longer offers sweet words, no need. I serve his needs — nothing, if not a good wife. As his desire fades, he blames my slackening flesh, strident tongue, faltering admiration,

my obsessive jealousy. And I am still useful; who could blame, if any dared, a husband seeking respite from a shrew who doesn't understand the burdens of godhead? When he's had enough, I give him a reason to go. He leaves only to protect them from my stalking. He should get some cards printed with his little farewell message:

'It's not you darling, it's that vicious old obsessive. She is dangerous and I can't take the risk of her hurting the one I love.'"

"Why not make an effort to be nicer, win him back from those little tramps?"

"Yeah make a fuss of him, get yourself a makeover?"

"You would handle it better, be the fresh taste he craves? Serve, serve and smile, is that your recipe? Every year, hoping to delight him, I renew my virginity, get my nails and hair extended, dazzle with designer clothes and diamonds, but I can't find a hopeful virgin heart or fresh belief to curve my mouth free of disillusion. I bathe in dew to make my skin sparkle,

but can't collect dewy dreams to shine in my old-wife eyes. So I hold on with angry claws, watch him coax those mayfly girls, reward them for what he never thanks me for giving. With scorpion words I try to instil fear, in nymphets hoping to shine in the reflected heat of power, seeking disposable pleasure. Fool's gold for very foolish girls."

"Sorry, Hera, that's another show: *'Gold diggers who crash and burn'*. Call if you're a young woman who has suffered trying for the good things, or if you're her mother, sister, or penniless ex."

DADDY'S GIRL ON THE COUCH

"Come in, Ms. Olympus, or may I call you Athena?"
"Athena. Olympus is just a convenience for the court. I never needed a *surname*.
Everyone knows who I am and who my father is."
"Well, Athena, what do you understand to be the purpose of this meeting?"

"Another of your little rituals! Some things don't change. I'm here
because you want to 'understand' my actions and make a report on them
to the court – as if a mortal could."
"You sound angry; do you want to talk about it?"

"You don't have a couch, so I assume you're not offering classical analysis.
We inspired Freud. Jung was influenced by our family histories, *if* they were
available, but you are such a short-lived species. If we'd endowed turtles or
redwoods with your monkey curiosity there might be some point."

"You feel my shorter life span makes it difficult to grasp your viewpoint?"
"Ah you are one of those humanistic types, person centred, so you don't have to
offer wisdom or insights. The lazy school of therapy – get your client to do all the
hard work and you sit back and take the credit or avoid the blame."

"I'd rather see it as respecting the wisdom of the person in front of me –
and with the goddess of wisdom sitting opposite?"
"Oh very neat. This might be amusing. Ask your questions then, I may answer some."
"Could you tell me what led up to the events that brought you before the court?"

"Before the court! Time was when no mortal would have dared, but the family feel –
that is the inner council of the firm – that we have to modernise, be seen to be more
accountable, pay taxes, offer conducted tours – that sort of thing. It has created
a disrespectful tabloid culture. Now any mortal thinks that we can be sued or prosecuted.

But since Zeus permits… The girl's mother was the complainant and the whole cause
of the problem. Her precious daughter had a small talent that she pushed and promoted
well beyond its limits. She won a lot of little local textile competitions, but she was never
going to achieve weather-girl status. Then this publicist stepped in, suggested controversy

to raise her profile. Her mother went on daytime television boasting that her daughter could
beat me. I ignored it, of course, but Zeus has got a tight little bunch of spin doctors peeling

his grapes and they thought it would be good for our new, softer image. So I did it. Uneven
contest from the start: I'd everything to lose in front of a jury of mortals burning to pull us down.

It was a fix, good television, allegedly – it's all in the angles and editing. I kept my dignity
till that woman did her victory dance and the reporter stuck his microphone in my teeth."
"You lost your temper. What did you do?"
"I exercised my rights, turned her daughter into a spider – but as a mark of respect called the species

after her and left her skills in perpetuity for her daughters. I thought that was only fair."
"If you were exercising your rights, why are you on trial?"
"Because of that hyena pack of journalists and their smear campaign. Zeus's advisers rejected
the thunderbolt solution; they said the focus groups reacted very negatively.

They felt submitting to a trial would demonstrate our new democratic godhead."
"Thank you, you have been very frank. That's the end of our meeting."
"Is that it? What are your conclusions? Why didn't you take a family history?"
"Your family history is well documented, but not necessary for this report.

My conclusions are for the court; your barrister will have a copy and will
go over it with you. But briefly: there are some unresolved feeling about mothers.
The changes in roles, expectations and cultural norms have had a strong effect.
Willingness to take a course in anger management, a self-esteem workshop

might be helpful – Paris rejecting your wisdom and influence, choosing a different
kind of woman obviously pained you. Addressing your problems, taking
responsibility for changing can be seen very positively by the courts…"
"Mothers! This case has nothing to do with mothers. I don't have any feelings

about mothers, I don't have any *issues about mothers* I never had a mother,
Zeus was father and mother to me."

THE THINKING WOMAN'S SOLUTION

Electra complex? Don't try that Freudian stuff on me; who do you think gave him the idea?
There's no comparison; her flawed father was mortal; we are weighed in a different scale.
I don't have, nor would I choose, the refuge of religion like that pious old maid cherishing
her fugitive father. Who'd want to marry a girl walked down the aisle by her father/brother?

Your lives are too shallow, your minds too fragile for that brew. In my case, you could trace
family of origin influences, make the connection with a woman swallowed by a husband's
needs and my personal commitment to achieving: majoring in hard sciences, military strategy,
medicine, architecture, civic planning – but still spinning like a good Greek daddy's girl.

I've studied the subject, analysed myself as goddess, daughter and woman – understood
the issues and resolved them. Of course, no man can measure up to my father, he's the god's god.
It doesn't mean I can't relate to ordinary men, just that my standards for a peer relationship
are hard to meet, but I've adjusted healthily by any measure: intimacy, commitment, productivity.

I've had many long and intimate relationships with men. Perhaps more mentor than girl friend
but full of commitment and passion for knowledge. Certainly not sterile. I feel we demonstrate
a thinking woman's answer to the career /children dilemma. I call it the seahorse solution.
I impregnate their minds. Men give birth to my ideas and raise them to maturity.

HYSTERIA, A HEROINE

Inspired by the Ancient Greek theory that the womb unanchored by pregnancy, floating up and disturbing the mind, caused female emotional instability. I wondered: If that were true, what happens when the anchor is no longer available?

Freed from duty, the vagrant womb moves lightly, for an organ of
her bulk. Though no longer blood rich, she remains well-connected,
heavily muscled, an ex-pro, determined not to run to seed. Those days
are done. All tears are dry for the lost, the almost, the never. So what

fortune can this traveller seek? Not much to pack, little for this champion
container to contain. No wonder she floats without effort to those thin-aired
regions, remote and cloudy, the mind of an older woman. Seeking a
new role, she roots and rummages; disturbing all routines she answers

incoming calls with contagious confusion, generating chaos. Among
dusty files, she learns of a fish, which in full age, transforms female to
male. Our heroine, Hysteria, declines the treat. Not dog enough to be
taught this particular new trick. Besides she has the gravest doubts.

Does the world really need another? Still searching, she finds inscribed
on a dusty mirror's rim the legend: "Function follows form". If that is true,
she muses, my options are much less than slim. Finally she pens an
optimistic wanted ad. "Ex cauldron, seeks new occupation. Experience

of nurturing, creative source, seed bed. Open to all and any positive
thoughts and ideas. Please reply." Ideas came. Half-grown, half-baked,
half-starved. All were welcomed. Hysteria reclaimed, recycled, redeployed,
becomes the mind's willing surrogate, gives birth to Athena's mortal siblings.

Note: The goddess Athena was said to have been born from her father Zeus's forehead.

HESTIA

i: Self-Contained

I do not spill confessionals over visitors' feet or
flood their ears, such narrow funnels, with my
wants or woes, rather accept their presence as
proof, silent answer to a question I do not ask.

My love, without ambiguity, spoken in acts, in
detail cherished, small needs anticipated, your
petrol tank filled, shoes re-heeled, towels deep,
soft and warm beside your bath. Half aware

bones murmur belonging, home. Kernel with
sleeping milky core. Unnamed, knows all names.

ii: Self-Completed

Within a central maze, solid stance, shielded
honey-wax candlelight licks my face into
chiaroscuro mask, but here is no mystery
except simplicity. The visible is secret, safe.

No one believes it is single ply. One thread to
run this maze. It begins in stillness, then
encompasses blood and breath; body's
humming hive, smoke-charmed, drowses.

Patience. Slow suffusion, rhythms alter as
cell by cell by cell, deep sweetness gathers.

A BRIEF STATEMENT FROM WOMEN'S PLACE

I am Artemis, Goddess of this place, in your terms perpetual head of state.
I will speak briefly. I don't do photo opportunities, soul-scraping interviews
or daytime confessionals. I will not answer any questions. This is sacred space, a sovereign state,
like the Vatican but much older. No men here, not even in joke or song or story.

Here in our wilderness, without footprint, tone or scent of man, great trees fall. Since no man can
hear the sounds which shiver our skins and fill our ears, do you imagine that there is silence?
I can confirm there was an incident involving a male intruder. He was quickly apprehended.
We dealt with him in accordance with our laws. The penalty for spying on our nakedness is death.

That is widely publicised. He was well educated, had leisure to hunt, was not blind or mad.
You call my justice savage? He was a man, not a stumbling innocent, no bewildered boy-child.
He knew my coverts, stalked my hunters, took with his eyes what is not for any man. He could've
closed his eyes, knelt blind and silent for mercy. Instead he fed his eyes with our flesh, then ran,

a thief, with those private images in his head, and hid. Did he intend to come back or just rerun
the film behind his eyes, fingering memory? An example – merciless, brutal – will be remembered.

GREEN SPACE

Green shifts, whispering with scents, rippling with sounds,
as light flirts, teases swaying saplings, caresses stolid trunks,
sifts leaves of their shadows. Movement maps the terrain, defines habitat.
Movement marks time. Stillness shapes the hunted, till safety is shattered

by the flight of an arrow, the thrust of a spear, the spring of a trap, the
tightening of a well-set net. Hunters are home. Fires are kindled for
the kill, bloody elbows gut, pluck and truss. Meat is celebration; prayer
prayer is hunger satisfied. Hair holding wood smoke, stray twigs,

detritus of the hectic chase, is soothed brushed and braided.
Pleasure is well-earned, aches eased with green-breathed oil pushed and
stretched into accepting muscles, glistening on warming skins. Sleep is
a smiling, silk-textured dream-sound tracked by green-tasting sighs.

He was a not-so-secret weapon and the enemy spin was so good our guys
were spooked by his rep — just one guest appearance booked for a battle field
and they'd run. So the men in grey got creative, looking for his Achilles heel.
A politician with a small town religious background? Hot sex is a safe bet.

They fed me the "Your country needs you" line. At first I thought they meant
a tour with some geriatric comic and last year's pop star. You know the gig:
flash your tits if you're patriotic, raise the boys' morale, remind them they're fighting
for the right to see forty-eight g on page three. They mentioned Mata Hari?

Public respect, the chance to make mainstream movies, Promised to take me
seriously. Said you can't be a page three girl for ever. Not all of you hit the charts
or marry footballers. I asked for expenses and an hourly rate not tied to results,
but should have read the small-small print. Delilah who? They never met me.

No movie, no medals. They let the tabloids loose. I went from being *Delilah,*
seventeen, forty-eight g, student hairdresser from Sorek Valley, (posing, boobs
out, holding a blow dryer) to *Philistine whore destroys naive golden hero.*
I was another cheap slapper who grassed-up her boyfriend. He was never that.

He was terrorist/patriot with no fashion sense, wearing untanned lion skin and
a yard of matted hair. No diamonds or even roses, just some sweet goo he found
inside a dead lion. He was the sort who cries all over a table-dancer, talks about
his wife and hates you next morning. He fell out with his bride on their honeymoon.

He left her at her father's for months without a word, then he turns up with a *goat*
as a make-up present. Sam thought sex was sin so didn't need studying, just
committing and regretting. I taught him a thing or two about pleasure — then he was
hooked. Sometimes I think he can't have been *that* stupid — perhaps he was just tired

of it all, the lion-slaying, the whole small-town, strong man, lorry-pulling, local-hero-
of-the-resistance bit. That's why he finally told me his secret. Three tries before I got it —
glad I'd negotiated an hourly rate, not the results-only package. He slept. His hair was
hacked off. Our guys took him. I shampooed my hair, had wine in a bubble bath.

I invested my money in a glamour modelling school while my name was still in the headlines. Occasionally, on anniversaries, it's dug up. *Where is she now? Scandals that shook the establishment, Fatal Love Stories of our times*: all the same programme. I always get paid up front, no freebies. I give good answers. Well-rehearsed quotes,

short and spiky – they like that. No one ever talks about my patriotism, only his. No one mentions his cruelty to animals. What cruelty? It was reported, but the spin was good. That young lion (notice they never say how young) that he ripped apart alive. Who remembers those three hundred foxes he tied together by their tails and set on fire to

destroy our crops? How fresh was that ass's jawbone he used to club a thousand men? They only ask about the sleaze. I say, "I was just seventeen." They ask about the sex. Not much to say about that. He's dead after all. They ask for intimate glimpses, little stories that show the man behind the legend. I had to think a bit the first time. Oh yes, like when

he beat up thirty men he didn't know and stripped them naked because he lost a bet. Were they our guys? Philistines, yeah, otherwise it would be ABH/GBH and theft wouldn't it? He had a bet at his wedding reception with thirty of his bride's brothers and cousins. The loser had to provide designer gear from boxers up, so he just picked

the thirty best-dressed men he could find, left them bruised, naked, no dry cleaning, tossed the stained kit to the winners. There is usually an awkward pause; after that they find a way to segue into how I feel about his death. Wasn't it a tragic ending? Yes for three thousand of us celebrating, thanking our god for victory. For Samson?

He won't be the last politician to bring the house down to cover his ruin. Maybe he was the first terrorist or a religious martyr, depending whose papers you read. He's safely sanitised in his tribal records, forgiven by his hardcore God, but I sometimes wonder how you'll remember me.

VOICES IN THE WILDERNESS
Genesis 15, 16, 17, 18 & 21

i

He spends our nights stargazing, comforted by their uncountable numbers. Everything has been said.
"I love you. It will happen when God wills." We have silence. His blind faith and my dumb despair
have been married so long we can argue wordlessly but not without bruising. Waiting has left my skin
loose on stiffening bones. She has tender skin, juicy fertility but can't afford children. I decide to expand

her job description. The variation is in her contract under "Any other duties compatible with the role."
I use my tired body to convince him. Clinch it with his sex's shrunken silent answer to my hand's question.
Don't notice how often she is called to his tent night, night-long. Don't ask this girl who sleeps with my
husband anything at all. Don't see the bright new scarf or hear gold chime on her wrists. Each pregnant

day cancels a decade of my life. She sighs my hand off, her eyes say *my child, old woman.* Small words,
bitten sighs, sharp silences he won't see; there's no arbitration, no applause for a hit, no sympathy for blood.

ii

Donkey-boy, that's what they call me where he can't hear. I am a second best son, but for thirteen years
all he has. The god who wanted my foreskin said I was born to the wrong mother, but I'd have hoards of
sons for dad's sake. Mum ran away when she was pregnant but an angel sent her back, saying I'd be a wild
donkey man falling out with everyone, even my brothers. She came back to give birth to me in Sarah's lap

so I could be *her* son too. But we all knew; it didn't really work. He loved her best. Mum was a mistake
excused by having me. Then the old bat got pregnant and I saw my mother shrivel waiting; but I thought,
my father loves me. The name-calling got to stone throwing; but only on the sly; the baby might die or be a girl.
We heard men rejoicing so we knew that she'd had a son. We stayed out of sight but everyone had to

be there for my little brother's weaning feast. *She* saw something in my face that upset her. My father's
eyes perhaps? Early next morning he came with food and a water skin. Told my mother, "You and the boy
must go." Turned and hurried towards *her* tent and their god-intended heir. I became a throwaway son.
My mother had been something to him. I never asked what he'd meant to her. We just walked to nowhere.

It didn't matter. No money, little water, less food, no shelter, just a slow way for us to die, leaving his
hands clean. Kinder if he'd had the guts to cut our throats, make a blood sacrifice to his god, as if he was offering
something he valued. I heard later that he did just that with my brother. It was a big deal, him being willing
to give his precious "only" son to god. I never heard that my brother protested, so perhaps he felt insecure in

our father's love too. After all if you can send your eldest son to die in the desert? When we'd had enough we lay down, separately. If you have no comfort to give or receive it is less painful to die in private. I was too old to cry in my mother's arms, too young for her to cry in mine. Then this angel came, pointed out a well we hadn't seen. Said even though I wasn't the full deal, Abraham's god would make me a father of

nations too. Silence while the angel looked, waited and I looked back. Said nothing. It seemed Abraham had kept me on his policy with modified cover. Mother said, "Ishmael, where are your manners? Thank the messenger for his time. It costs nothing to be polite." So I did. But I never said that I believed in *this* big daddy's consolation prize. Anyone know where can I get a refund on my premium for only-son cover?

iii

They say I laughed at the messenger. I suppose it would sound bad to say I was hysterical, shaking with something, let's call it laughter, biting my tongue not to say what I'm sure God could have read in my heart any time in the last forty years or so; if he'd been looking. Seasons reverse and Abraham wants me again and our son is born. If we die who'll protect him from that Egyptian and her son? With my tongue

back in my control, I want that girl and her stopgap son gone. He refuses. I know he must be sure of a son; sucking babies often die. I wait till my son is weaned. Abraham is all misty gratitude, presses me to name a gift. I don't want flowers, I want them gone. He tries to reason with me. Next will come anger and if he actually says no, he won't change his mind. I use the weapon I'd sworn to leave buried in Egypt. Change

the subject. Ask what is the name for a man who gives his young wife to another man to buy his own safety, tells her, "Say you're my sister." Takes payment in goats? They leave a silence that we never quite fill.

iv

I am barely a sketch of a character, a shape to hang a situation on. No motivation, no dialogue. Who'd hear? If they could have had a womb on legs I wouldn't have been named. No words but I get to be screwed and screwed over. I get to run away and run back. I get to meet an angel. But he never asks me anything, only points the way back to captivity, tells me my son will be a wild donkey surrounded by brother enemies.

I provide a son for them. Nothing for me. Silence from the script for the next thirteen years. No directions, no movement. I'm just backdrop. Then the third act; exit, stage left signed to the wilderness, carrying my son. Has the director forgotten that he is thirteen, not a babe in arms? I carry him till I fall, cradling his body burning dry. Then bells, lights and Hallelujahs, an angel pops up like a demon in panto pointing to the well

of sweet water I'd so plausibly overlooked. In the absence of dialogue or direction I decide to make some business to flesh out the scene. I find my son a wife to root him in his culture, like me she is an Egyptian.

FOR A GOD BETRAYAL IS ONLY A BREATH AWAY.

I returned. My journey had been measured only by will.
I had been away, how long? I had already counted to five million decimal places.
I returned and saw her hands on his head, making tender cups, for soft, new-cut bristles.
His young arms, straining to contain her deep sighs, his chin blurring her vermilion parting.
Red throbbed. Blinded me. My hands found blade and steel sheered between them.
His head, a child's ball at her painted, pampered feet.
"Our son!"

ii

There was a moment of dazzling pain, head and body separately parcelled.
A bright ball fringed with fraying tendons, eyes startled open,
rolled to dabble ochre-painted feet in sudden scarlet!
Dust puffed in small flares of alarm, before being doused in blood.

iii

I have never yearned for my father's godhead, only his presence;
single-mother goddesses are very hard to leave. She had grown
accustomed to our joint reflections in the still water of her days,
she would not picture a solitary self in that silent mirror until
its glassy surface was shattered by a bright ball.

iv

No. I will not lift that curtain. Not even to draw dusk across day.
Since the ochre snakes on my feet were dyed sudden sticky rust, I have never repainted them.
Without red powder, my parting shines ivory pale, since vermilion flowed into my hair.
No. Not even to sweep dawn over dripping dew, I will not look through *that* window's memory.

v

Gods do not err, but they can make amends. I promised the head of the next being I saw.
God-words are granite on the tongue. We are bound by the clanking weight of their smallest echo.
The young tusker came with a sound of muffled drums. It is a new beginning, not open to comparisons.
A broken vessel, flawlessly restored, is still less than it was. I thought it better make to make a God.

vi

Elephant youth is moving from grey-bouldered safety, that constant trunk to tail
connection with mother, to be fussed by aunties, or bossed by older sisters practicing.
Elephant youth is long days of chewing, wringing reluctant sweetness from grass,
yearning for leaves, which must be sweeter. Months of watching those moving mountains,

the old bulls. Trying their shoves on each other, fencing with the tusks we almost have.
Measuring our bulk because one day... "One day," the aunties say, "You will leave us.
All males do, when it is their time to wander." And all my whys and whens only got
"When it is time, you will know."

And one morning, the mango's turpentine stinging sweetness, it's hairy fronded
seed was not enough. One morning, the rising bubbles of bird's song were sunk
beneath a red-stained tide of scent, steaming from the softening sex of my sister/cousins,
flowing, weighting air with lust.

The push and lean with the other boys had an edge like aloes. The big tuskers looked
smaller, as if one day they could be taken — and, on a breath, bigger, as their desire reddened,
saw not a bull calf, but a rival. The aunties were right; I did know the time to leave.
We moved away, eating the sappy leaf-bunched branches, which were sweet and ours now.

We left dangerous appetites behind and moved towards our strength. Surgical thrust of
tusk, python strength of trunk, percussion that asserted our presence on the jungle floor.
Everything ended with a God's promise. My head for his son's empty shoulders.
Perhaps he had no aunties to tell him, "One day, boys must wander."

The simple hungers of young males helped us to a language; the body's growlings
gave us a rosetta stone. Like and not like being conjoined twins. Years of different
kinetic memories, skin-and-bone deep assumptions of identity built into thought and
desire. Locked into each other, sharing the helpless straining for impossible distance.

We finally stopped bruising against the bones of our prison, learnt that some things
just made our brains bleed. We stopped trying to push each other beyond the limits of
our shared skin; began negotiations for shared movement, memories bleeding, blurring.
We'd both been mother-raised, ambivalent towards a distant shape of adult male.

Pre the pivotal moment, one of us had been saying a hard goodbye while the other,
blindly savouring freedom, blundered into a family tragedy. Poor timing all round.
So an eternity of pointless infighting or find the limits of this new state — a no-brainer
of a choice, unless you have a taste for stale sick. Better be a God.

Even imposed godhead has its freedoms, its intrinsic choices. Power is built into the
contract but the charities you choose to sponsor, the kind of God you are, those details —
like the family photos or hardy plants in a cubicle office — those you get to choose.
Best avoid the possibility of role confusion, being subsumed into or becoming just

another avatar of an established god, a small town mayor wearing the president's name.
So we worked out what we wanted — food and sex, of course — slowly compromised on what
turned us on, then things flowed into a wider taste-band and we both got some surprises:
eternity of satisfactions, without sanction or limit and a close buddy to share it all.

We lived every adolescent male fantasy and found the need to stretch muscles and
powers even if only to add new savour, to remind ourselves of wanting, playing at
waiting, to keep the juice fresh. No heavy philosophical debate, we just decided to go
with our strengths — food and fun — and major in new things; no heavy ear-bashings, no

being the god on call for martyrs, no being fast-bleeped for miracles just when you're
in the mood to chill. We didn't present it that way, of course, we played the modesty card.
"You have the serious stuff well covered, but we want to pull our weight. We thought
we could handle gates and doorways, make new starts lucky, that sort of thing."

It went down well; we'd avoid treading on any venerable toes and, of course, new projects
have less built-in boredom, no norms to be measured by. So that's us, the Elephant-headed
god, a fun guy for laughs and luck. No complaints, no petitions, no weeping or wailing.
New beginnings and gateways that lead into them, that's our remit. We added a spice of luck.

Don't bring us tears or sad stories. Too much salt is unhealthy. A shining crystal on
a crisp-baked cracker is acceptable, no bitterness bottled or preserved, but if you must, a
drop of bitters to prime our tongue for luscious morsels. We are a god of happy appetites.
Laughter and good food fill our days: soft, butter-rich rice, shoveled into cloudy mounds,

scented with cinnamon and rose, cooked in green coconut milk, served on rustling but
still sappy palm leaves. We live our only sermon. Things happen, even to a child of gods
or an Eden-innocent animal, so why not to you? It happens; then you get to choose: eat bile,
blind yourself with tears or walk through the gateway with open eyes and call on us.

v

Movement restrictions are still in force, but
I know sheep, study them, even dream them,
could discuss qualities of wool, technicalities of
sheering, pasture and parasites, breeds, colours,

configuration... Have posters with Romney Marsh,
Jacob's, no not Herdwick, too coarse a fleece,
even as lambs, for my touch. Oh yes, I can cut
a single sheep from the flock, direct it to a pen

of my choice. Have an instinct for the weak or
vulnerable. Form a good rapport; they feel safe
with me. I've cultivated that, know what they
crave: tenderness, the sense of being protected,

valued. I give them that; they go where I choose.
Modified restrictions are still in force, so I will
stay close, watch a lot of television. Cookery
programmes. Read too. Simple recipes are best.

Fresh ingredients, little garnish. Not overcooked:
softly pink, still juicy, even rare. Surprising how
many share my tastes. Spring-sweet flesh. Never
see mutton advertised now. Not doing any harm.

Just looking. Butcher's shops are on every high
street, quite legal. I am just looking. Flesh. Raw.
Sweet. Tender muscle. Bones full of soft brain-
flavoured marrow, ready to be sucked out,

relished between teeth. So my appetite is really
mainstream. Except I like mine with blood
still pulsing, wool rough under my tongue,
between my teeth tearing, but I'm just imagining,

doing nothing wrong, only slowly ruminating,
salivating. Thought fed, hunger gnaws. Grows.

BURNING BRIDE

Birds of varied plumage and disparate habitats, we hover over dusty ground,
wings winnowing, eyes pecking, ready to snatch and squawk. Wanting that
death to have glittering resonance or juicy entrails to pick over. Needing her
to be more than a girl burnt alive on her husband's fire. Scolding starlings rant

about abuse, a flock's easy short-cutting of complexity for bone-values. Patriotic
eagles soar into flights of religious or regional renewal, looking to hatch a phoenix
from her ashes. Magpies and mynas seize glittering opportunities to make a hot
documentary or raise hawkish profiles, appearing incensed on chat shows. Sparrows

take a dust bath and prepare a stall to sell paan and souvenirs. Bulbuls sing patriotic
songs to enrich their record company. Strange, there are no vultures among us, though
we all want to count her as a bird of our own plumage and song. But all we have is ashes,
dulling feathers, weighting flight, gritting lids – and an unspeakable smell glazing tongues.

ADAM EXPELLED

A fresh start away from men's fists.
I'd found too many. Ran with my baby
doors slammed behind me. Found
sisters and a dream .Discovered Eden

Eve run. Toddling Adam answerable
for fallen Gods in his image. What is
he doing here? Baby rats are pink, and
helpless too. *He* will be a *man* in this

women's space. Snake voices whispered
salvation he could never find. Evil was
chromosomal. Adam half-man fled hell.
Bought oblivion till he found obliteration

GENDERED CHOCOLATE

The double x'd are simply banned, but can you be too gay
for chunky chocolate?
The ad-man's chosen recipients: clench-jawed, darkly stubbled
lost boys, yearning
for aproned Wendies, framed in fifties' certainty, set up to play
real boys games.
Buying this solid sweet is a reassuring shorthand for working class
masculinity,
straight-edged, blue-wrapped. A thick phallic treat to fill in till Wendy
lays on tea.

TOUR

Here they come, the dispirited, disgruntled, or just
plain dissatisfied, and it's my job to change all that.
Perspective and positive thinking in one prescription.
How their feet smell. I usually have a little rant about that.

The first time, I worried that I'd blown it. Not provided
the uplifting experience that was contracted for. But the
verbal flagellation was a hit, had them sniffling in the
coach all the way home. Got a few touching letters about

how they were using pumice stones and verruca cream
with a new sense of privilege. So the bosses agreed to
change the script. One of them even wrote a paper on
interactive attitudinal challenge – or something like that.

Here they come, and I raise my trousers to display my
plasticised tib and fib ends. "Capped, if you must know,
for hygienic display. Not many footless European men
available, that's why I was 'conscripted' for the PHS.

I continue to answer the predictable questions; I never look
them in the eye, (it embarrasses them and reduces the tips.)
Never listen. Always some worn-out wit looking for an argument
so he can say, "But you haven't a leg to stand on."

Usually some brash boy wondering aloud if I have to sit to
pee, and whether I can still have sex standing up. Smile with
understated cheerfulness and see them visibly inflate as they
make the comparison, filing back onto the coach light-footed,

grateful. I'm off to the *Bull and Bear* tonight. They are featuring
"The man allergic to Viagra". That should put a spring back in my step.

CLIFF TOP MUSEUM

Secure above the uproar of waves, I curate a cliff-top hamlet,
awed by what slow decay reveals of social bones, roof trusses
the family had forgotten, "A" frames of secrets, horsehair that
gave body to plaster, embedded with fragments of oral history.

I dust and smooth lavender-breathed beeswax over the worn
surfaces as structures draw nearer to the inexorable edge. I don't
offer protection from watermarks or mould — only the reassurance
of daily dusting, weekly airing of those empty, half-floored rooms.

I accept gappy windows with their erratic reminders of time and
toileting. I savour the footnote consolations of a social historian
and the pressed flower pleasures of archaeology. These have
never been my homes. We encourage visitors. I explain that we

gently conserve with tenderness for the precious materials
that we cannot restore, but the visitors still weep, facing blanks
where cherished images once hung. They stand mute, rain snaking
down their necks, clutch white-fisted a key that no longer opens home.

SELF SCOURING WINDS

Howl down memory, twist, distort her stance into a defensive bow, all arrows spent.
Lost but still seeking, she walks carpeted sameness, walks, and never arrives.
Surrounded by the kindness of hourly strangers, she accepts with patient dignity all
indignities of our intrusive necessity. Smiles. Gentle drifting on the moment's tide.

Soft nightlight to keep dark at a manageable distance. Sun rises in the eyes of others,
a warmth not quite held by memory. She expands in love she cannot frame or
set in context, only reflect and magnify, in selfless return without restriction.
Empty-handed receives with open-handed grace. In the vacuum of self becomes love.

MIRROR IN WINTER

The shining present tense of her smile hangs dew-strung,
cobwebs circling her smooth gummed mouth. Seconds pass
and illusion too, leaving canals of Mars drought-cut across
the delta of her face. Spare hawthorn twig against December's

longest night, one day's weight could snap her bones. There's
beauty; I wonder which morning she woke to that eroded
landscape, unblossoming desert, and owned it. Will I smile
in that dew-strung shining tense, that must become my present.

LAST BEST GIFTS MISCHIEF.

Never a long thinker, a man of body filled with mischief.
He has kept a lad's simple humour; confined, he declines
the sterile dignity we assign to age. Mischief comes
readily to his stiffening hands. Simple slapstick.

Small ambushes set to shake the dignity of his carers.
He sleeps? Beneath a rakish cap eyes gleam, plotting.
Lacking materials, he contrives. Lets the budgie loose,
disturbs the goldfish, startles grandmothers into girlie giggles,

races his wheelchair, ruts and rucks the carpet and brings
a spice of risk to bland corridors. Pulls the tablecloth out
from under the teacups, but not until he's drunk his tea.
He's going down with his ship, offering a rude salute.

THE LAST CHRISTMAS JUMPER

Knit and pearl, the yarn catches on the coarse skin of her finger
where she has been darning rips in the fabric of the universe.
Her fingers are slowing, stitches slip, not always in pattern, but
she rather likes the random loops – a surprise in making is a treat –

so she incorporates them into her work, producing a texture like
fleece. It looks odd beneath the picture-knitting of creation, but
could link, perhaps, with the lamb motif above; besides, it's the
thought that counts – it will have to – her thickening knuckles crack

as her fingers flex. No more jumpers in six days; this may be her
last handwork and she begins the casting off of her creation.

REAL BULL

Highland cows are unashamedly shaggy.
No Lady Shave for them, they cluster protectively
about their bull. Hostile, they lower skean-dhu
horns as we pass between their field and the A9.

They know his value; he's the real thing, not white
coated "Was that it?" fertility, but hay-breathed
sandy, dreadlocked, real male. Hot sex, weighted
with satisfying tradition. In their protective huddle,

he's a flower child among amazons in harvested fields,
where giant digestive biscuits of wheat wait for a tea break.

GREEN EXECUTIVE STRESS

Thumb-sized solitary bees, the ultimate non-team players, wearing post-ironic, football-strip jerseys, thrust their thrumming furred bodies clumsily into blossom after blossom, "Wham, bam, hope you fruit up, mam. Gotta get every flower seen to, there's a fertility quota to exceed", while the breeze carries the March winds' order, fifty percent of the Mayflowers' contract, on a non-negotiable deadline.

You should see the penalty clause for late delivery. The deadline presses, March into April, memos swirl in their wake: buzz-blow-flutter-hum-huff-hover-murmur. Daylight must be extended, consumers' expectations rise with each success: a more floriferous display, a heavier fruit set; last spring's records must be broken. Flying high, they pop spring's green bubble-wrap to relieve their type "A" executive stress.

PROZAC FOR THE PAIN OF BRICKS AND BARK

Insecure glass no longer trusts its embedding;
wood distracts itself by observing the trees.
Muted by moss they stand dripping depression.
Withdrawn from the therapeutic squawks of

foraging corvines in love with their insights,
plucked raw from the intestines of domestic
collision. And still cold tears run unconsoled
down half-warm windows rattled by winds

that turn solid walls to shivering. Where is
the Prozac for the pain of bricks and bark?

ANNUNCIATION: TO STARGAZER LILIES

During their long convent-bound noviciate, close folded green habits properly conceal
their weekly sprouting leaf-flounced limbs. They stand meek and meditative maidens,
sealed from all the buzz and blunder of our spring. Slowly the pressure of their soft white
thoughts thins well-washed habits into transparency. They have kept custody of the eyes.

Lined garden corridors, modest, downcast, closed to all except infusing spirit, that impulse
to open the tender self to July. A flaming vocation far from the timid religion of evergreen
Sundays and bark chipping paths laid on weed-suppressing membrane, or the bloodless
spirituality of raked gravel rivers and crane-assisted natural rock formations. Their worship

requires surrender to the spirit, laying bare every gram of pollen-self, accepting the winged
messenger who announces that they have been chosen. Will some refuse, elect safe sterility?
No, each makes an act of faith in an unformed future. Openly professed brides, they become
earthier, no less devoted, but somehow more relaxed and intimate with their shared spouse.

These Lily-nuns, with sauce on their white habits, hand rolled cigars of terracotta-pollen
in fingers of yellow streaks, abandon themselves prayer-tranced to their bridegroom sun, offer
him the incense of their ripeness, magnifying his generosity with their own, asking nothing
from the gardener content with their vows to bear a personal death and next year's hope.

OFF-PITCH SCORING

See the soft land reaching towards that starred wave dreaming of melting
into its touch. Tender land lies prone beside the lipping lapping wave, dizzy
with the football moon brazening the sky. Fresh friable shore opening gently
to that first-chosen, dancing sweat-slicked wave, wanting to touch six-packed sea..

We always score. We share the game, we share the score and then need more.
After we score we play and score again. On any turf we always share the score

Pressing, pulsing, pausing, pawing, pounding, grinding her supine shore as
another and another and another wave crests on the rockless land, and rain
lashes, catching her earthskin between relentless teaming waters till she's only
mindless mud and aching sand, an empty beach after the final goal is scored.

We always score. We share the game, we share the score and then need more.
After we score we play and score again. On any turf we always share the score.

"It's only natural violence," say the scavengers harvesting her sea-wracked
shores, undefended land that lay so naively alongside mindless oceans, open to
empty-minded skies. The gulls judge; "She should have known what to expect
from macho rain and star-glazed seas teaming under a brazen football moon.

We always score. We share the game, we share the score and then need more.
After we score we play and score again. On any turf we always share the score.

RETURN OF THE ALL SINGING, ALL DANCING TIMBER WOLVES

A rich wind plays welcome and we move past the plastic flags of human anxiety towards the rhythms of waiting prey. Our bodies know we've only lacked partners and a floor for the music which has played through our dreams. We've always heard the songs, but now the lyrics are blood-ripe in our mouths. Our breathless audience provides the drumbeat, follows our performance, as if each dance

could be a grand finale. We're a new company with traditional values, offering guest soloist opportunities to the local population. Not everyone makes it past the audition, but we regularly talent spot. We're really keen on equal opportunities; you could describe us working to redress the balance. Most of our guest dancers are disadvantaged or disabled or disaffected in some way. We work hard to integrate them

into our company; it's a package deal: dancing and community service. We harmonise acapella our first long song after our first sequenced dance. We've already eaten the trophy. The deer, rabbits, elk form our repertory. Without barres we hone our choreography. They haven't seen dancers like us in generations; we're the headliners; every other act is just supporting. We show coyote-critics their place.

Then an air so fat-rich, wrapped in a week's worth of sweet strong muscle, an ocean of blood in shaggy fur. Like rediscovering a legendary song cycle, now we must recreate a dance lost in dust: new/old patterns of run and turn, a troop of fresh steps and pas de deuxs. With leaps and lunges we make partners of these movable feasts. Earth has held the archival echoes of this musical we revive to critical acclaim.

Thunderous applause; the audience deeply moved; the critics beside themselves, waiting to dissect and gnaw the bones. The after-song we raise to the remembering moon completes a blind and knowing balance.

WHERE NILE CROCODILES SLEEP, WAITING FOR TEARS

Somewhere an African nation, its name sonorous with regret, is lit
with your perpetual smile, a gauze curtain over trembling movement.
You are glad of these little lives, adapted to your constant brightness by
rotating feet or sheltering in sharp shadows, holding breath for moisture,

reserving their hunts for the bloodless detachment of your polar dreams.
Rain is a rumour you refuse to hear, though frantic flowers, the brisk/brief
rivers with short-shelf-life breeding pools would curve softer smiles into
your heat-glazed face, but you glare down the hint of grey tinged clouds.

Barely alive, hidden from your dry eyes, each in its carrel under the sands,
waiting, you hear their slow, oiled hearts oozing life through cold leather veins.

HORROR STORIES FOR THE LONGEST DAY: BEWARE MEN CARRYING TORCHES

This is the longest day, time for hanging close, clustered like grapes,
hearing tales that make wings tremble and ears swivel for danger. Beware!
They come crunching, moving over ground like beetles, their grumbling
voices bruising the walls. Like earth moving, they come into our roosts;

faces shelled in hard plastic, hairless bodies wrapped in strange slack
skin, they come shredding our dark. Men the dung diggers. Once they
used to scrape our floors to buy their food, make fortunes from fertility,
now they come to lengthen their names. They come to weigh, to nick,

to spy our routes and map our desires. They come stealing our songs,
envying our wingspans as they strain to hear our singing without tape
or tool. I suppose they are jealous. We are living winds with all soft wide
darkness to ride, skies of crisp-bodied broad-winged insects to harvest.

They can only fly wrapped in metal sealed from sensation. Our ears are
fine-tuned to the slow earth stories running through our days' dreams,
whispering of seeping water and the seasons of stone. Oh children, beware
the soft, hairless night-blind day-crawlers; beware men carrying torches.

NOW EUROPE IS TO SET THE WOODEN HORSES FREE

(Recent European legislation could make traditional rocking horses "Unsafe")

How will we rehabilitate/re-skill them back into the workforce?
Investigate redundancy or early retirement packages? Set up
a commission? Hold an enquiry? We conduct aspirational
interviews with the soon-to-be redundant Dappled Rockers.

They seem at a loss for alternative career options. Have they
lost themselves in children's cries, forgetting to yearn for wind
to lift their manes, flies to exercise their tails, the pungency
of dung to prove their life? Do they dream of food or foals

or the bite of desire? We offer brown belt retirement pastures
or private plastic surgery pre redeployment as fairground
workers. Our offers are rejected. They dream of rootedness,
solid as their parent trunk, weathered free of gaudy colour.

They dream of standing deep, reaching high, as slow years
renew shredded bark while twigs raise themselves from dead
wood, crowning their victory with green flags. They leave our
neverland and dream, not as toys but as those remembering.

VOYAGE OF THE YELLOW FLOTILLA

Sea shifts half-conscious from colour to colour, not able to wake
from under cotton-rich sky or sink deep enough to dream fleets of
ducks brightly bobbing and becking, barely weighting the waves.
No dream required; they have supplied their own. And made it true.

Smug red lips pout *I told you so*. If Eddie the Eagle can fly without
wings, why should we be limited to toddler's tubs, cat nibbled soap,
slimed bystanders. Sardine-packed indentured /migrant workers, we
never signed the contract for endless smiling immersion in tepid scum.

Five years domestic labour was agreed to repay passage and arrangers
fees, then our feathers would break through and we'd our find seaway.
We heard the crew laughing, taunting us with the truth. Plastic has no
right to grow beyond human use or dream more depth than bath-time.

Our prayers to Poseidon answered, storm released, we form a flotilla to
follow that old call towards our summer tides. We map long suspected
secret superhighways, currents so subtle it takes our light hearts to ride.
Pure scientists, we don't expect recognition from skin-wrapped minds,

don't hold our smiles waiting for a fellowship or publication of our
report in *New Scientist*. *National Geographic* does a photo essay but none
of us are interviewed. If you'd only known, we'd have been fitted with
radio collars like timber wolves reintroduced to their ancestral habitat.

What mapping opportunities you've lost, thinking that any yellow duck
must be from our shipwreck. After all, "Once you've seen one bath duck..."
But there are other less-heralded and older voyagers among us. River
duck races expect losses; one or two brave escapees make it to open sea;

over the years, handfuls quietly taking the underground railway. Who
counts their ducks once their chicks have grown beyond bath time?
Sometimes a child heard the flightless dream and set the dreamer free,
lost on a seaside holiday. We meet them, seafarers still, smiling buoyant,

glad to greet others of their kind after years of trying British Duck Signs —
bill shake, tail flick, head up, tail up, nod — on unreceptive gulls. No storm too
harsh, we were made for neglect, rough handling, smiling wide-eyed optimists
who yearn for rough waves, while you run a tepid bath with baby bubbles.

WE ARE THE GARLIC GIRLS

They thrust their bursting booties, barely held in splitting seams, in your face. Don't ask
about roots. They are indifferent to the globes clustering supportively beneath the surface.
The grannies have had their day. Let them rest in the dark, befriend the keel slugs and play Bingo.
We are the stars of our own *Now*, dying to show our tightly-packed petals. We could be rear

of the year. Our music is a fusion: street-crushed garlic garage-house; it's not for the timid.
Ours is out in your face, full-bodied, sweaty singing. Oh how the paparazzi will hound us.
No avoiding the price of fame. They will fly any distance to snatch a moment of our day.
Not our fault we're hot, but there's nothing between us and that B-Band; its all hype. Perhaps just

a *Hello* moment, but *OK* have bought the wedding photos, the *Daily Mail* have an exclusive
on how we made it/lost it/drugs and pregnancy/break up/solo-flops/comeback. Garlic girls? Who?
The slugs are setting up auditions for next year's crop. If they can survive that slimy
process, the globes are funding another fame-school, looking for next year's new taste.

TURKEY DOCTRINE

(Inspired by the contents of a "Healthy Eating" sandwich. "Layers of smoked reformed turkey and pastrami complemented by mild mustard and sliced gherkins in a soft plain bagel." 297 calories. 5.0 grams fat)

Precise calorie and fat count, I should feel more grateful.
But I prefer the illusion of succumbing to impulsive appetite...
So what is between the slices?

Smoked turkey, bubble-skinned pickled memory adding bite to the present and hot lipped
Italian-American pastrami, just controlled by the primly butterless bagel. Mmmm. No
Wait, what was that again? Reformed turkey? I don't want my meat repentant. Heathen is
juicier, without the stale-bread mustiness of regretted sins,

but the religious requirements of hunting and plucking are, like dancing naked
under the moon, not suited to our climate. Orthodox turkey, with the full jewelled ritual
and rite of scarlet wattle and antiphonal gobble, is a moister option. But
I fear any monotheistic belief. What if this is a turkey martyr, dying in faith,

believing his virtues – restrained gobbling, moderate preening – are about to be rewarded
by becoming one with the Deity? Does that elevate me to being
the Turkey-God? May the non-turkey-god forbid, the meat in that sandwich
might turn me vegetarian. No. Give me an unrepentant, unreconstructed gobbler of life.

An "I regret nothing" turkey who tossed his comb, spread his tail feathers wide, swung his
wattles with pride, and strutted his stuff,

till he got stuffed.

A CALL FOR RESPONSIBLE PUBLICATION.

There is a crisis. Too many writers are producing uncommissioned cats.
The first attempts raise fluffy sentiment but soon grow into flea and mite-
infested manuscripts skulking in alleys, rootling in creative writing classes,
entering competitions, stalking slush piles. Unfledged writers preying on

the minds of publishers' assistants, warping them by the sheer weight of
unsolicited cat baskets whose inhabitants fill corridors with the smell
of stale litter and the sound of meows demanding urgent feeding.
A one line impersonal rejection is the safest, any more could encourage

the stray to expect adoption – contract, meals, publication. How many
strays can one publishers' reader home? They have their own pets to
edit, groom for the Frankfurt show. One caring solution is to limit
breeding/writing to those homed by responsible agents or publishers.

Writers are for life, not just for holiday best-seller lists. To control feral
population, bait traps with vanity and sterilise unsanctioned talents with
constant indifference. The alternative is that cats that outgrow their
kittenish appeal are brutally discounted, abandoned on motorways or

stranded in small towns without bookshops, without publicity or marketing
strategies or even shredded as an act of mercy to prevent a miserable
warehouse-bound fate. Pedigree cats, written to guidelines, furless to protect
agents from allergies, declawed for the safety of the publishers' upholstery,

have an ever narrowing gene-genre pool adapted to their market niche, but
if a solar flare of taste caught these publishing giants, all imprint and formulae,
unprepared for a talent winter, where's the wild flexibility to rebuild a writing
population when all the flea-bitten tabbies, rubbish-raiding gingers, swaggering

and scruffy black and whites have been neutered to protect them from the harsh
disappointment of market forces? Who will bring you disturbing mice to read,
eviscerate issues despite your squeamishness, tangle your thoughts in difference,
scratch complacency, remind you that human is just one perspective, not the only view.